T0070672

11 EASY STUDIES

by J. B. Duvernoy (Op. 276) and J. F. F. Burgmüller (Op. 100)
for Piano and Orchestra

Edited by
Gero Stöver

DOWANI International

Contents / Contenu / Inhalt

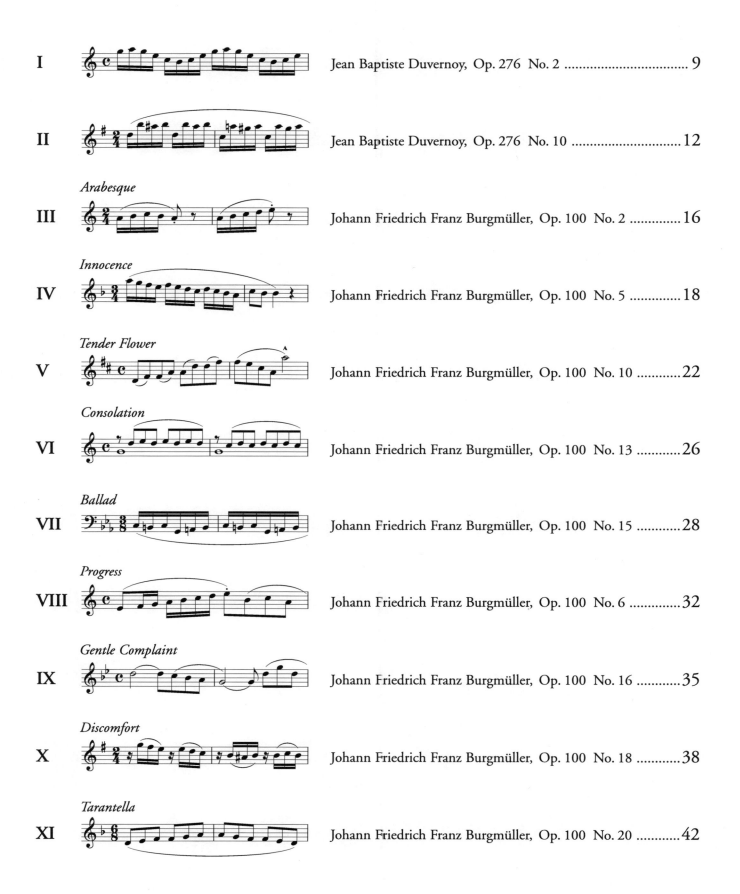

Preface

With this edition we are pleased to present you something entirely new in the field of piano teaching: the premiere publication of well-known piano studies by Duvernoy (Op. 276) and Burgmüller (Op. 100) with *orchestral accompaniment*. The inventor of the *DOWANI 3 Tempi Play Along* series, the pianist and teacher Drazen Domjanic, hopes that this practical edition will give all pianists the impetus and motivation they need to practice studies on a daily basis. Practicing studies is a very important part of the training of every music student, learner, amateur and professional. These newly arranged orchestral accompaniments to well-known studies give rise to miniature piano concertos, thereby turning the practicing of studies into an entirely new experience and a source of enjoyment, especially for beginners.

The orchestral arrangements and piano reductions are the work of the pianist and arranger Gero Stöver, who has masterfully combined subtle orchestral timbres and expansive string writing with the rather simple harmonies of the studies. Concerning the musical text, the pieces are relatively easy to play. This enables you to focus entirely on the music and to hear and grasp it consciously. *DOWANI 3 Tempi Play Along* offers you an ideal starting point for this.

The CD opens with the concert version of each study, that is, the piano part with orchestral accompaniment. Your first practice session should be in the slow tempo. If your stereo system is equipped with a balance control, you can practice the right or left hand separately by adjusting the control. We refer to this form of slow, separate study of the left or right hand as *PIANO TRAINING*. In the middle position, both hands can be heard at the same volume. If you do not have a balance control, you can listen to each hand on a separate loudspeaker. After you have studied the selection in the slow tempo, you can advance to the medium tempo and further refine your playing. The piano reduction of the orchestral part assumes the role of a professional pianist. Having mastered this practice tempo, you can now progress to the original tempo with orchestral accompaniment. At both the medium and original tempi, the piano or orchestral accompaniment can be heard on both channels (without solo piano) in stereo quality. The studies have been sensibly divided into subsections for practice purposes. You can select the subsection you want using the track numbers indicated in the solo part. Further explanations can be found at the end of this volume along with the names of the musicians involved in the recording. More detailed information can be found in the Internet at www.dowani.com. All of the versions were recorded live. To shorten the distance from the CD to the experience of live music-making, we offer all orchestras a complete set of performance material, including a conductor's score.

The fingering in the solo part of our edition was provided by Sabine Krüger, a piano teacher who studied music education at the Folkwang Hochschule in Essen and took a performance degree in piano from the Detmold-Münster Musikhochschule, where she studied with Professor Gregor Weichert. Today Ms. Krüger teaches piano at the Folkwang Music School in Essen, where she also heads the Pianists' Forum.

Piano teaching has made very great progress in recent years. Many piano teachers have their own ideas, theories and experiences, especially with regard to fingering and the use of the pedal. Nonetheless, we have decided to add fingering to our revised new edition, for experience has shown that many learners, especially those encouraged by play-along CDs, want to play new pieces without their teacher's knowledge. The fingering in our volume will enable enthusiastic learners to prepare a piece without the aid of their teacher, but without coming to grief with ill-considered spur-of-the-moment fingering combinations. Moreover, it gives teachers an opportunity to assign pupils a new piece without wasting valuable lesson time in writing out fingering. The aim of our fingering is to achieve a smooth delivery and to concentrate on the music itself. In cases of doubt, we have taken the physical features of children's hands as our guide. The fingering added by Sabine Krüger lay no claim to absolute truth, but are intended merely as suggestions. It goes without saying that teachers are completely at liberty to write down fingerings of their own.

We wish you lots of fun playing from our *DOWANI 3 Tempi Play Along* editions and hope that your musicality and diligence will enable you to play the concert version as soon as possible. Our goal is to provide the essential conditions you need for effective practicing through motivation, enjoyment and fun.

Your DOWANI Team

Avant-propos

Nous sommes heureux de pouvoir vous présenter, avec ce recueil, une nouveauté mondiale dans le domaine de la pédagogie instrumentale pour piano : la première édition d'un recueil d'études connues pour piano de Duvernoy (op. 276) et Burgmüller (op. 100) avec *accompagnement d'orchestre*. Le créateur de la collection *DOWANI 3 Tempi Play Along*, le pianiste et pédagogue Drazen Domjanic, donne avec cette édition pratique une impulsion et une motivation nouvelles à tous les pianistes en ce qui concerne l'exercice quotidien des études. Le travail des études est un élément très important dans la formation musicale de chaque élève, étudiant, amateur et pianiste professionnel. Avec de nouveaux arrangements pour accompagnement d'orchestre, les études connues ressemblent à des concertos pour piano en miniature. Ainsi le travail des études deviendra une expérience d'un type nouveau qui apportera aussi beaucoup de plaisir aux débutants.

Les arrangements orchestraux et les réductions pour piano ont été réalisés par le pianiste et arrangeur Gero Stöver qui sait très bien lier des images sonores subtiles et des grands mouvements pour cordes aux structures harmoniques relativement faciles des études. Le degré de difficulté des morceaux choisis se situe dans la catégorie "facile". Vous pourrez ainsi vous concentrer entièrement sur la musique pour bien l'écouter et la comprendre. La collection *DOWANI 3 Tempi Play Along* constitue pour cela un point de départ idéal.

Le CD vous permettra d'entendre d'abord la version de concert de chaque morceau (piano avec accompagnement d'orchestre). Votre premier contact avec les morceaux devrait se faire à un tempo lent. Si votre chaîne hi-fi dispose d'un réglage de balance, vous pouvez travailler soit la main gauche, soit la main droite en réglant la balance. Nous avons appelé ce travail séparé de la main gauche et de la main droite *PIANO TRAINING*. En équilibrant la balance, vous entendrez les parties des deux mains à volume égal. Si vous ne disposez pas de réglage de balance, vous entendrez chaque main sur un des haut-parleurs. Après avoir étudié le morceau à un tempo lent, vous pourrez améliorer votre jeu à un tempo modéré. La réduction pour piano de l'accompagnement d'orchestre sera jouée au piano par un répétiteur professionnel. Quand vous maîtriserez également ce tempo de travail, vous pourrez jouer avec l'accompagnement de l'orchestre au tempo original. Vous pourrez écouter l'accompagnement joué au piano ou par l'orchestre à un tempo modéré et au tempo original sur les deux canaux en stéréo (sans la partie soliste). De plus, les études ont été divisées en sections judicieuses pour faciliter le travail. Vous pouvez sélectionner ces sections à l'aide des numéros de plages indiqués dans la partie du soliste. Pour obtenir plus d'informations et les noms des artistes qui ont participé aux enregistrements, veuillez consulter la dernière page de cette édition ou notre site Internet : www.dowani.com. Toutes les versions ont été enregistrées en direct. Pour que le pas entre le CD et le concert ne soit pas trop long à franchir, nous proposons à tous les orchestres le matériel d'orchestre avec conducteur.

Les doigtés dans la partie soliste de cette édition proviennent de Sabine Krüger, pianiste et pédagogue. Elle fit des études de pédagogie instrumentale à la Folkwang Hochschule Essen et passa le diplôme de pianiste au Conservatoire Supérieur de Musique à Detmold/Münster auprès du professeur Gregor Weichert. Elle travaille aujourd'hui comme professeur de piano à l'école de musique de Essen et dirige le "Forum pianistique" auprès de cet institut.

La pédagogie instrumentale pour le piano a beaucoup progressé au cours des dernières années. De nombreux professeurs de piano ont leurs propres idées, leurs théories et leurs expériences, surtout en ce qui concerne les doigtés et l'utilisation de la pédale. Nous avons tout de même décidé d'ajouter des doigtés dans cette édition révisée, car l'expérience a montré que beaucoup d'élèves – surtout grâce aux éditions avec CD – souhaitent essayer de jouer des nouveaux morceaux à la maison sans professeur. Les doigtés dans notre édition permettent aux élèves motivés de préparer un morceau tout seul sans échouer devant des combinaisons de doigtés irréfléchies et spontanées. De plus, cela offre aux professeurs la possibilité de donner aux élèves un nouveau morceau à travailler, sans être obligé de noter des doigtés pendant les cours. Les doigtés proposés visent un jeu raffiné et une concentration maximale sur la musique. Dans le doute, les doigtés sont adaptés à l'anatomie de la main d'un enfant. Les doigtés de Sabine Krüger ne prétendent pas détenir la vérité mais s'entendent en tant que propositions. Chaque professeur de piano est, bien évidemment, libre de noter ses propres doigtés.

Nous vous souhaitons beaucoup de plaisir à faire de la musique avec la collection *DOWANI 3 Tempi Play Along* et nous espérons que votre musicalité et votre application vous amèneront aussi rapidement que possible à la version de concert. Notre but est de vous offrir les bases nécessaires pour un travail efficace par la motivation et le plaisir.

Les Éditions DOWANI

Vorwort

Wir freuen uns, Ihnen mit dieser Ausgabe eine Weltneuheit auf dem Gebiet der Klavierpädagogik vorstellen zu können: die erste Ausgabe bekannter Klavieretüden von Duvernoy (op. 276) und Burgmüller (op. 100) mit *Orchesterbegleitung*. Der Erfinder der *DOWANI 3 Tempi Play Along*-Reihe, der Pianist und Pädagoge Drazen Domjanic, gibt mit dieser praxisorientierten Ausgabe allen Klavierspielern neue Impulse und Motivationserlebnisse für das tägliche Üben von Etüden. Das Üben von Etüden ist ein sehr wichtiger Bestandteil der Musikerziehung eines jeden Musikschülers, Studenten, Amateurs oder Profis. Die neu arrangierten Orchesterbegleitungen zu bekannten Etüden lassen Klavierkonzerte im Miniaturstil entstehen. Dadurch wird das Üben von Etüden zu einem ganz neuen Erlebnis und bereitet vor allem auch Anfängern große Freude.

Die Orchesterarrangements und Klavierauszüge stammen von dem Pianisten und Arrangeur Gero Stöver, der es ausgezeichnet versteht, subtile Klangmalereien ebenso wie ausladende Streichersätze mit den harmonisch eher einfacheren Strukturen der Etüden zu verbinden. Der Schwierigkeitsgrad dieser Stücke liegt im leichten Bereich. Somit können Sie sich ganz auf die Musik konzentrieren und sie bewusst hören und verstehen. Dafür bietet Ihnen *DOWANI 3 Tempi Play Along* eine optimale Ausgangsbasis.

Auf der CD können Sie zuerst die Konzertversion eines jeden Stückes (Klavier mit Orchesterbegleitung) anhören. Ihr erster Übe-Kontakt mit dem Stück sollte im langsamen Tempo stattfinden. Wenn Ihre Stereoanlage über einen Balance-Regler verfügt, können Sie durch Drehen des Reglers entweder nur die linke oder nur die rechte Hand separat üben. Diese Art des langsamen und getrennten Übens von linker und rechter Hand haben wir *PIANO TRAINING* genannt. In der Mittelposition erklingen beide Hände gleich laut. Falls Sie keinen Balance-Regler haben, hören Sie jede Hand auf einem Lautsprecher. Nachdem Sie das Stück im langsamen Tempo einstudiert haben, können Sie im mittleren Tempo Ihr Spiel weiter verfeinern. Den Klavierauszug des Orchesterparts übernimmt dabei ein professioneller Korrepetitor. Wenn Sie auch dieses Übe-Tempo beherrschen, können Sie mit Orchesterbegleitung im originalen Tempo musizieren. Die Klavier- bzw. Orchesterbegleitung erklingt im mittleren und originalen Tempo auf beiden Kanälen in Stereo-Qualität (ohne Klavier solo). Die Etüden wurden in sinnvolle Übe-Abschnitte unterteilt. Diese können Sie mit Hilfe der in der Solostimme angegebenen Track-Nummern auswählen. Weitere Erklärungen hierzu sowie die Namen der Künstler finden Sie auf der letzten Seite dieser Ausgabe; ausführlichere Informationen können Sie im Internet unter www.dowani.com nachlesen. Alle eingespielten Versionen wurden live aufgenommen. Damit der Schritt von der CD zum Live-Erlebnis nicht fern ist, bieten wir allen Orchestern das komplette Aufführungsmaterial inklusive Partitur an.

Die Fingersätze in der Solostimme dieser Ausgabe stammen von der Klavierpädagogin Sabine Krüger. Sie studierte an der Folkwang Hochschule Essen Instrumentalpädagogik und absolvierte an der Musikhochschule Detmold/Münster die künstlerische Reifeprüfung als Pianistin bei Prof. Gregor Weichert. Heute ist sie als Dozentin für Klavier an der Folkwang Musikschule Essen tätig und leitet das „Pianistische Forum" am selben Institut.

Die Klavierpädagogik hat in den letzten Jahren sehr große Fortschritte gemacht. Viele Klavierlehrer haben ihre eigenen Ideen, Theorien und Erfahrungen – vor allem in Bezug auf Fingersätze und die Verwendung des Pedals. Trotzdem haben wir uns dazu entschlossen, in dieser revidierten Neuausgabe Fingersätze zu ergänzen, da die Erfahrung zeigt, dass viele Schüler – insbesondere durch die Play Along-CDs – den Wunsch entwickeln, neue Stücke ohne das Wissen des Lehrers zu spielen. Die hier notierten Fingersätze sollen es ermöglichen, dass ein begeisterter Schüler ein Stück ohne das Zutun seines Lehrers vorbereiten kann, ohne dabei an nicht überlegten, spontanen Fingerkombinationen zu scheitern. Des Weiteren gibt dies dem Lehrer die Möglichkeit, dem Schüler ein neues Stück aufzugeben, ohne vorher im Unterricht Zeit für das Notieren von Fingersätzen einzuplanen. Die hier angebotenen Fingersätze zielen auf geschliffenes Spiel und die Konzentration auf das Musizieren. Im Zweifelsfall orientieren sie sich an den physiologischen Gegebenheiten der Kinderhand. Die von Sabine Krüger angegebenen Fingersätze erheben keinen Absolutheitsanspruch, sondern dienen als Vorschlag. Natürlich steht es jedem Lehrer frei, seine eigenen Fingersätze zu notieren.

Wir wünschen Ihnen viel Spaß beim Musizieren mit unseren *DOWANI 3 Tempi Play Along*-Ausgaben und hoffen, dass Ihre Musikalität und Ihr Fleiß Sie möglichst bald bis zur Konzertversion führen werden. Unser Ziel ist es, Ihnen durch Motivation, Freude und Spaß die notwendigen Voraussetzungen für effektives Üben zu schaffen.

Ihr DOWANI Team

I

C Major / Ut majeur / C-Dur

J. B. Duvernoy (1800 – 1880)
Op. 276 No. 2

© 2004/2005 DOWANI International

DOW 17001

II

G Major / Sol majeur / G-Dur

J. B. Duvernoy (1800 – 1880)
Op. 276 No. 10

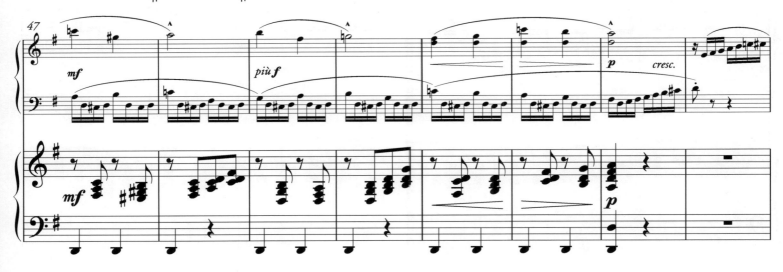

III

Arabesque / Arabesque / Arabeske
A minor / la mineur / a-moll

J. F. F. Burgmüller (1806 – 1874)
Op. 100 No. 2

IV

Innocence / Innocence / Unschuld
F Major / Fa majeur / F-Dur

J. F. F. Burgmüller (1806 – 1874)
Op. 100 No. 5

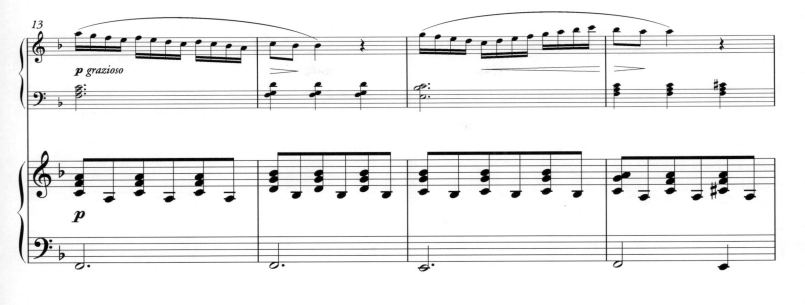

V

Tender Flower / Tendre Fleur / Zarte Blume
D Major / Ré majeur / D-Dur

J. F. F. Burgmüller (1806 – 1874)
Op. 100 No. 10

VI

Consolation / Consolation / Trost
C Major / Ut majeur / C-Dur

J. F. F. Burgmüller (1806 – 1874)
Op. 100 No. 13

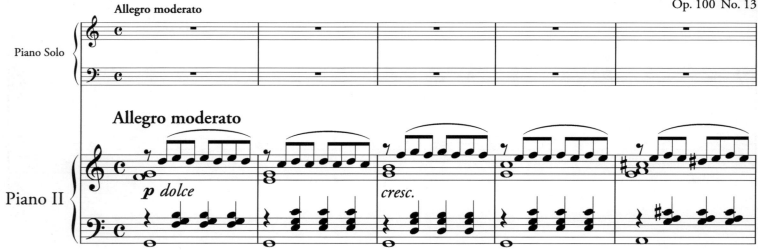

VII

Ballad / Ballade / Ballade

C minor / ut mineur / c-moll

J. F. F. Burgmüller (1806 – 1874)

Op. 100 No. 15

DOW 17001

VIII

Progress / Progrès / Fortschritt
C Major / Ut majeur / C-Dur

J. F. F. Burgmüller (1806 – 1874)
Op. 100 No. 6

DOW 17001

IX

Gentle Complaint / Douce Plainte / Sanfte Klage
G minor / sol mineur / g-moll

J. F. F. Burgmüller (1806 – 1874)
Op. 100 No. 16

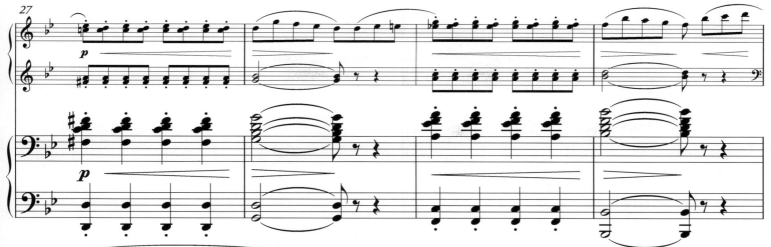

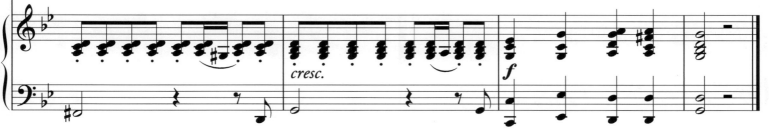

X

Discomfort / Inquiétude / Unruhe
E minor / mi mineur / e-moll

J. F. F. Burgmüller (1806 – 1874)
Op. 100 No. 18

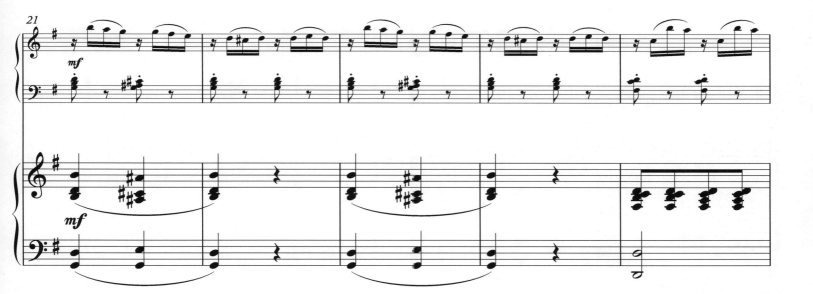

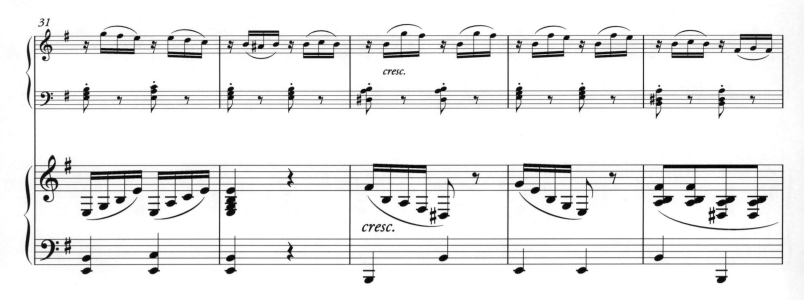

XI

Tarantella / Tarantelle / Tarantella
D minor / ré mineur / d-moll

J. F. F. Burgmüller (1806 – 1874)
Op. 100 No. 20

43

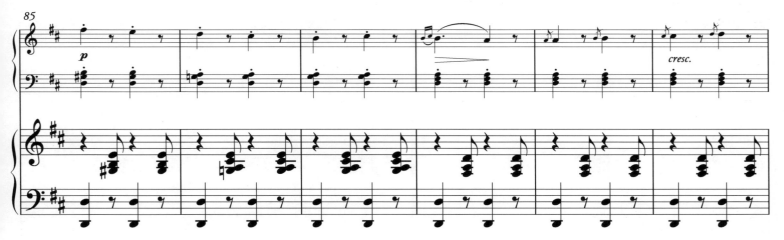

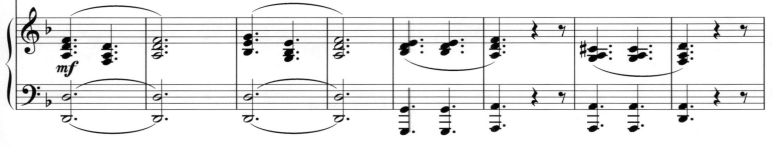

ENGLISH

DOWANI CD:

- Track numbers in circles
- Track numbers in squares

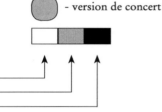

- concert version

- slow Play Along Tempo
- intermediate Play Along Tempo
- original Play Along Tempo

- Additional tracks for longer movements or pieces
- **Double CD:** CD1 = A, CD2 = B
- **Concert version:** piano and orchestra
- **Slow tempo:** channel 1: left hand; channel 2: right hand; middle position: both hands at the same volume
- **Intermediate tempo:** piano accompaniment only (piano reduction)
- **Original tempo:** orchestra only

Please note that the recorded version of the piano accompaniment may differ slightly from the sheet music. This is due to the spontaneous character of live music making and the artistic freedom of the musicians. The original sheet music for the solo part is, of course, not affected.

FRANÇAIS

DOWANI CD :

- N° de plage dans un cercle
- N° de plage dans un rectangle

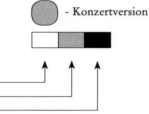

- version de concert

- tempo lent play along
- tempo moyen play along
- tempo original play along

- Plages supplémentaires pour mouvements ou morceaux longs
- **Double CD :** CD1 = A, CD2 = B
- **Version de concert :** piano et orchestre
- **Tempo lent :** 1er canal : main gauche ; 2nd canal : main droite ; au milieu : les deux mains au même volume
- **Tempo moyen :** seulement l'accompagnement de piano (réduction pour piano)
- **Tempo original :** seulement l'accompagnement d'orchestre

L'enregistrement de l'accompagnement de piano peut présenter quelques différences mineures par rapport au texte de la partition. Ceci est du à la liberté artistique des musiciens et résulte d'un jeu spontané et vivant, mais n'affecte, bien entendu, d'aucune manière la partie soliste.

DEUTSCH

DOWANI CD:

- Trackangabe im Kreis
- Trackangabe im Rechteck

- Konzertversion

- langsames Play Along Tempo
- mittleres Play Along Tempo
- originales Play Along Tempo

- Zusätzliche Tracks bei längeren Sätzen oder Stücken
- **Doppel-CD:** CD1 = A, CD2 = B
- **Konzertversion:** Klavier und Orchester
- **Langsames Tempo:** 1. Kanal: linke Hand; 2. Kanal: rechte Hand; Mitte: beide Hände in gleicher Lautstärke
- **Mittleres Tempo:** nur Klavierbegleitung (Klavierauszug)
- **Originaltempo:** nur Orchester

Die Klavierbegleitung auf der CD-Aufnahme kann gegenüber dem Notentext kleine Abweichungen aufweisen. Dies geht in der Regel auf die künstlerische Freiheit der Musiker und auf spontanes, lebendiges Musizieren zurück. Die Solostimme bleibt davon selbstverständlich unangetastet.

DOWANI - 3 Tempi Play Along is published by:
DOWANI International
A division of De Haske (International) AG
Postfach 60, CH-6332 Hagendorn
Switzerland
Phone: +41-(0)41-785 82 50 / Fax: +41(0)41-785 82 58
Email: info@dowani.com
www.dowani.com

Recording & Digital Mastering: Pavel Lavrenenkov, Russia
Music Notation: Notensatz Thomas Metzinger, Germany
Design: Andreas Haselwanter, Austria

Concert Version
Vitaly Junitsky, Piano
Russian Philharmonic Orchestra Moscow
Konstantin Krimets, Conductor

3 Tempi Accompaniment
Slow:
Vitaly Junitsky, Piano

Intermediate:
Vitaly Junitsky, Piano

Original:
Russian Philharmonic Orchestra Moscow
Konstantin Krimets, Conductor

© DOWANI International. All rights reserved. No part of this publication may be reproduced, stored, in a retrieval system, or transmitted in any form or by any means, electronic, mechanical, photocopying, recording, or otherwise, without the prior permission of the publisher.